HE'S NOT GONE

We do continue on

By Carol Oschmann

from Aunt Carol

a bit of Oschman folklore – but true.

Author's Tranquility Press
MARIETTA, GEORGIA

Copyright © 2022 by Carol Oschmann.

All rights reserved. No part of this publication may be reproduced, distributed or transmitted in any form or by any means, including photocopying, recording, or other electronic or mechanical methods, without the prior written permission of the publisher, except in the case of brief quotations embodied in critical reviews and certain other noncommercial uses permitted by copyright law. For permission requests, write to the publisher, addressed "Attention: Permissions Coordinator," at the address below.

Author's Tranquility Press
2706 Station Club Drive SW
Marietta, GA 30060
www.authorstranquilitypress.com

Ordering Information:
Quantity sales. Special discounts are available on quantity purchases by corporations, associations, and others. For details, contact the "Special Sales Department" at the address above.

For more copies, you may reach (866) 411-8655 ext. 106.

He's Not Gone/Carol Oschmann
Hardback: 978-1-958554-16-6
Paperback: 978-1-958554-15-9
eBook: 978-1-958554-17-3

Dedication

To Jim, I thankfully look back to the many conversations we had about what we wanted to do in our next life. You were unwavering in two things, you would fly fighter jets. In this life you had an extensive knowledge of airplanes, often amazing your best friend, John, who was in the air force. You could look up in the sky, when planes from Mac Dill Air Force Base flew over and tell me what kind of plane it was. Then again, how was I to know? We talked of friends long gone who we planned on seeing. I hope this made passing easier for you. My goal was to give dreams to people on earth. Secondly, you were sure we would meet on top our favorite pier in St. Petersburg, Fl. The pier's gone now. Let's hope it had a soul and that soul is in heaven also. We'll meet again there, many times, I'm sure.

Love, Me

I humbly suggest that the time has come to rethink our beliefs about an afterlife. As director of the Shared Crossing Project, I have had the privilege of being able to review and study more than eight hundred separate SDE cases. Our research shows that a benevolent afterlife awaits us all at the other side of deaths door.

William J Peters
Micheal Kinsella, Phd
"At Heaven's Door

John 3:15 "that whoever believes in Him should not perish but have everlasting life."

The New Kings James Bible

HE'S NOT GONE
By Carol Oschmann

By now you've heard of NDE's (Near Death Experiences – those things that happen when people die on the operating table and come back and tell of strange happenings). You may have also heard of SDE's (Shared Death Experiences where you travel part-way with someone who's dying). Well, my story starts with an SDE - or maybe the night before.

My husband was diagnosed with a deadly cancer and his doctor said he had only five or six years left to live. So, we moved back up North to be near our children, which also allowed him to spend one summer getting to know our great grandchildren.

When it became inevitable that he could no longer go on, we made him a bed in the living room and had round-the-clock nurses, thanks to our oldest son who hired them. Our daughter gave up her job and spent most of her time with my husband, his nurses and me. He was loved and we (or rather I) have been reaping the rewards – if you can imagine rewards in a situation like this that so many go through and are completely devastated with grief. I live in awe and wonder as each night brings me another visit from Jim. When he started taking me back to Heaven with him to meet loved ones who passed after he did, I knew I had to put this all down on paper for others to know it does happen.

Let me give a little background for those of you who don't know us. I've been doing dream work for more than forty years, dreamed for other people more than four hundred times (you'll see some later), taught dream interpretation in a prison, and have led many dream groups. I've given many speeches and sermons, and written four books about dreams. Jim has always been my cheerleader. He wished that my work would get the recognition that he, alone it seems at times, felt it deserves.

I think its best if I show you my dream diary with some explanations inserted so you can understand as you read this. Our beloved Jacobus Marinus (Jim) passed in the wee hours of November 23, 2021. For a couple of days before that, he communicated only with people he alone could see, and held the conversations in his native language, Dutch. To say that he was already gone was not a stretch.

November 22, 2021

Dream: Jim, a young boy and I were about to board an airplane to fly to Rochester. We got into a disagreement and Jim and the young man left without me. I raced around the airport looking for him. Two lines led to the planes boarding ramps. I asked if either plane went to Rochester. The answer was that the one going there had taken off already. Now what? Did he leave a ticket for me?

Meaning: I knew the next morning that Jim, through our dreams where we seemed to be sharing a connection not available during the day due to his physical condition, was preparing me for the fact that he was leaving me – by dying. Both young and old Jim were leaving which explained the presence of the young boy in the dream. I was more frantic in my dreams than I was in life. My daughter, Sue, was there supporting me emotionally as was the hospice nurse. I could only watch and take in the care they were giving him. I tried. One time as we were trying to move him to a more comfortable position in bed, he pointed his finger at me shouting "YOU," - then pointing at his recliner, he shouted again, "SIT." I did. If he left a ticket for me, I'm ready to use it anytime.

November 23,2021

I was alerted by the night nurse that Jim had passed. I don't know at what time. She woke me at 5AM. She'd already washed his body and readied him for the hospice nurse to come and declared him gone. I did, however, remember a dream. This is the Shared Death Experience that I spoke of earlier. Reading the next dream, readers , I hope, will understand Jim and I were tired of the dying thing and left the bed together.

Dream: Jim was in bed dying. I sat on the bed talking to him. He said he was tired of this dying business and I agreed. He got out of bed and we started doing things together. One thing we did was to visit an old man who rented space in a shack in the woods. The man wrote amazing stories. We brought him out of the shack and into the world so his work could be better known.

Meaning: The first sentence, so true. We were both tired of this dying business. My hopes for the rest were that the old man hidden in the woods was my writing and speaking about dreams. Despite doing this for a long time, I was barely selling any books. Maybe from the other side, Jim could better help me bring my work out into the open so many others could hear the amazing tales I had to tell. One could only hope. The dreams seemed to say that Jim was hoping this also. The truth was, that he was sick of feeling ill, trips to the hospital, having constant nurses at home (although I thank God and Jim Jr. for them). He was ready to move on. We'd seen him talking to his loved ones on the other side and heard his conversations spoken in Dutch several times.

November 29, 2021

Dream: Jim has picked out a new car for me. I haven't seen it yet but am secretly hoping for a convertible. It's been three days since he promised it to me. I take the note with the dealer's name and phone number on it. The operator is having trouble locating my car with the serial number I give her. Its four numbers that start with a 9.

Jim takes the phone from me and tries to solve the problem. I\we are getting frustrated. I suddenly see four new numbers, 8383. Where did that come from? I ask Jim. He gives the new set of numbers to the operator (who works for the dealership) and she finds those numbers on her computer. It's now 7:30 at night and I fear it is too late. But Jim says, "No - get dressed, we will have the car tonight."

Meaning: A new car for me. A car represents your life's journey. He's already given me a new persona by making me a widow. A new journey, indeed. I was hoping for a convertible – leave it to me not to be satisfied. Perhaps we are talking about my role as an author and speaker. That sounds much more flashy. When dealing with numbers in dreams, one train of thought is to add them together. 8383=22=4. Four signifies the four corners of the earth, completeness, - and hard work. Taken singularly, eight is the power to be, potential for success, wealth, and balance.

Three is the trinity, great strength, completion and creativity. Anyway you cut it, they're promising numbers!

The lateness of the hour refers to my old age and that I can still handle the life's work that I chose (or rather, that chose me)?

December 2, 2021

Dream: I'm wanting to join the choir of a new church. The choir was bigger than the audience. It made a semicircle, like a horse collar, with the top up high. I got to the top and a young boy does too, and, together we tumble over the edge into the snow. Each member of the choir wore a necklace made of ice cubes interspersed with diamonds. Several were lost in the snow. The boy and I sifted through the snow finding the diamonds along with some ice cubes. The others were quickly melting. We were heroes then and I found a bench higher up where four people sat to be highlighted at certain points in the service. I knew there must be a way up there, I finally saw the steps that led there and figured out the order of the procession. First, the four that sat highest, then the choir. It looked like you had to go through the choir to get to them.

Meaning: The new choir, the new church I want to join has to do with my wanting to join the people whose books are successes. Not only do I want to join them, I want to sing in the choir, be the highest one in the place. Taking this dream to my dream group, they decided the diamonds were my memories of Jim, the melting cubes represented my life, not quite all gone.

December 3, 2021

Dream: Our big dog was dying. It had shriveled up to the size of a bug and started acting nasty. It would bite you if you went near it. Jim and I fled the house and frantically looked for help among our neighbors. We knew even a phone to call the police would help, but had no luck finding a phone.

Dream number two: I left California ahead of Jim. We drove separate cars. In Philadelphia they were having peaceful diversity rallies. When I got to Rochester, they were also having peaceful diversity gatherings. My phone was nearly dead.

I asked my several neighbors to let me use their phones to call Jim. I desperately wanted to talk to him. My long-time friend, Hope, said I could use hers but she needed to change the battery first. We couldn't make it work so I asked other people as they sat and listened to the speakers and sang peaceful songs. No luck. Their phones were not familiar to me or even to them. I woke up but tried hard to go back to sleep and contact Jim. No luck – and then it was 7 A.M.

Song on rising: Songs often invade my dreams. A song on waking answers the question foremost on my mind in the dreams I just had. In this case it was trying to reach Jim.

The song: *I'm Back in The Saddle Again* (an old Gene Autry song.) I wondered – where did that come from? It had to be from Jim. I looked up the words and they're all about freedom. For him, no more pills, blood transfusions or obeying doctors' demands. He is free and telling me not to try to contact him. Time will show that he will contact me whenever I need to know he is all right. Actually, he is more than all right.

Meaning: Little did I know, at that time, but our nephew in California and our niece who lived outside Philadelphia, would both pass on before the following spring. The big dog turned ugly and got them.

Hope is the name of the friend for whom I first dreamed. She taught me that I could dream for others. Not even she can help me now, although she and I have recently reconnected and she is coming to Rochester where I live, for a visit. All the looking for a phone signifies the lack of communication, my not being able to call on Jim whenever I want to.

December 4, 2021

This morning (the morning of the funeral) I woke with no dream but a song, *On The Wings of a Snow White Dove,* He sends his pure sweet love, I took this as a sign from above, on the wings of a dove. Those words repeated all day in my head and I knew Jim was not gone. He was sending me love. Several days later, when Sue and I visited the monument company to pick out a headstone for our joint graves, she wanted a windmill to commemorate Jim's heritage, and I chose a dove for the other side to commemorate our love.

December 7, 2021

The funeral for Jim is over. It was three days ago I fell at the grave site and fractured two ribs. Jim Jr. ordered his younger siblings not to leave my side. So, David and Susan have been sitting with me ever since.

Dream: Jim and I sold our home on the island. The new owners came to see it, before we moved out. They could not back out of the sale. I took a walking tour with the woman and pointed out stores, banks, office buildings, talked of quick passage to Canada, the prison, and then I got lost. We kept on walking, hoping to find a familiar place so that I could call Jim to come and get us.

At 3:30 A.M, I woke in a lot of pain. I took pills and got something to eat and tried to go back to sleep at 4:30.

Meaning: The meaning of this dream was that I was proud of the life I had to give up. There is no island, unless you think of that poem by John Donnes, *No man is an Island Entire of Himself.* There is a prison in my dream work and the title of one of my award-winning (but not selling very well) books. I taught women in a Florida prison to understand what their dreams were telling them. The chaplain there said it changed many lives from the first meeting we had. I did that for three years and my book *Finding Spirit in Prison Inmates Dreams,* tells their stories. Dreams can be a great rehabilitation tool. The dream began with my giving up that life and ended with me, once again, searching for Jim, my deceased husband.

This morning I told David and Susan to please go home. I didn't need constant watching. I would be careful, no reaching, no picking something up off the floor. Just please go home and they gratefully did.

December 14, 2021

Dream: We are preparing to sit down and consume a feast. We are using the bed as a table. We move it a few times to get the best spot in the room. The benches for seating will be my old hope chest, and similar pieces of furniture where more than one person can share a seat. We take the tops off them and find cushions to sit on to be more comfortable. We finally get it right and settle, waiting in for the food to be served.

Meaning: The meaning of a feast, according to the Islamic dream dictionary is that worries will be over and joy and ease will return. It can also mean a reminiscing about the past, a renewal of past celebrations, reviving a state of joy, release from prison or freedom from debts. Google says when you dream of beds, it can represent a form of spiritual sanctuary. I hope I am bringing this to other people. What a beautiful dream!

December 27, 2021

Dream: The person in charge trained us in combat. I was to sneak up on an enemy, and fire my big gun while another one on my team came from another direction. I'd seen this in action before and knew it was meant to trip me up, put me and my teammate in the hospital. I contacted him, and we made a secret plan to avoid the war. Next, I was visiting people in the hospital and gloating with my teammate that we weren't hospitalized too. It wasn't us.

Meaning: A teammate is someone you support or who supports you. Jim is my teammate. Jim and I are gloating over our win. We got through this part of his life's war without getting hurt. He didn't want me to grieve.

January 2, 2022

Dream: I'd had a couple of dreams with no meaning other than wilderness areas and wars. Perhaps the wilderness areas were the loneliness I'd feel and the wars were referring to my way of fighting off those feelings of loneliness.

In this night's dream I'm driving Jim and the owner of a small food business to work. Jim gets dropped off first. He could not remember the route. He kept telling me wrong turns to take. Feeling he'd be late, we stopped and got the other man's phone out of the backpack in the trunk of the car. Jim couldn't remember the phone number to Mr. Parker at Kodak where he worked. I finally recognized the street. I wondered if Jim was feeling well, strong enough to go to his job. We stopped in front of the office. The boss, Mr. Parker, was lecturing on plants and regions (like the desert) where they grew. I said Jim could pass that test easily. But the boss was also doubtful of Jim's ability to come to work.

Meaning: I believe this dream was telling me that Jim was not strong enough yet to help me (from Heaven) with our earthly projects. I prayed harder for him to find his way in Heaven, and he would be at peace. Could our love keep him warm?

January 4, 2022

All these dreams of weakness and war might have been telling me to use my own spiritual powers.

Then a man called me out of the blue, having read one of my books, and he wanted me to dream for him. He had a lot of decisions to make that year which would impact his entire life. I hadn't dreamed for others in a while, but I agreed.

The next morning I called him and read him the dreams. He kept saying, "Wow, wow, wow! I wanted to know what I'd seen from his life. He said I saw his three children and the icy atmosphere of his home. He was contemplating divorce. But now he saw a festival of coming events if he just held on. He said that I had given him his answer. He thanked me and that was it. One more dream off into the dust of my memory with good changes in his life, and into the pages of my dream diary.

January 10, 2022

Dream: Balloons popping, leaving fingerprints on things. I feared the cleaning lady would make them disappear. I wanted to keep them.

Meaning: The balloons bursting reflected my daytime fears. The fingerprints are my memories. I wanted to keep them forever. Then again, every action leaves a trace.

January 13, 2022

Dream: My house is being remodeled. It's impossible to live in. My group (family or projects) go next- door to my elderly grandfather's house for shelter. He will take them all in except me. A Spanish lady finds me towels and cautions me to keep the tub dry because that is where I'll sleep.

Meaning: Jim is telling me that my life is still being remodeled. He's still working to help me from the other side. Sleeping in a tub is sure a new experience. I can't wait to see what he's coming up with. I have said yes to showing of my book, *Finding Spirit in Prison Inmate Dreams* in three places One is in New Jersey, at a book show, another is at the McGuire Air Force base in New Jersey for six months and then it'll be shown at someplace in Alabama as part of a book show, also for six months. I'm opening the doors that I can afford.

January 23,2022

Dream: Jim and I have performed a play. Three people, two men and a woman, approach us wanting to take the play to a neighboring country. We agreed, but must fly in a private plane. We fly low over islands, and can see very few are inhabited. Jim and I wonder if we'll remember our lines. In the plane, Jim sits side-by-side with people while I sit with my back to them.

Meaning: Jim is keeping up my hopes. I need to have faith although I can't see where we are going.

January 29, 2022

Dream: I am a rock – smooth, round, and flat, - lying with a lot of like-shaped rocks. We're tightly packed together and there is a layer of rocks below us. Something is causing the rocks to crack. I use my mind energy to stop the rocks from cracking.

Meaning: This sent me into a meditation of sorts. I put the word rocks in the center of a circle and then put every connection I could think of to the word 'rock'. What stood out the most were the words that Jim had been my rock, someone to lean on. I also had ageless, shoreline, hard, solid. You can try it yourself. For the word crack I came up with release, insides revealed, broken, barely a finger- hold. Or it could point to a relief in my publishing woes. One can only hope.

I wonder about my own spiritual energy. Is it needed in a joint venture such as Jim, in Heaven, and me, on earth, putting together a story or book such as this, or selling the books that I have already written? You'll see in the three dreams for other people what I had a chance to do before the month was over.

February 12, 2022

Cindy asked me to dream for her, to find out what her job in Heaven would be. Cindy is a close friend. I know a lot about her. I rely on learning something about the person I'm dreaming for to verify God is really talking to me. First her job. She has done dream work for several years. She's also a trained meditator. She has been given much direction in her own dreams to lead the best life possible, to accept the hardships and various problems with the people in her life. My dreams for her led us to believe she would be a greeter in Heaven. She'd be, for lack of a better word, an angel, who greets souls entering Heaven. As for the thing I didn't know, we both laughed when I read the part to her about jumping at sudden noises. She said that was so true. Just that day, she had yelled at her husband for slamming a door and scaring her,

Then I went through a dry period as I tackled living with my diabetes and leg pain.

February 26, 2022

Another friend, Robin, asks for a dream. She is another member of my dream group. She also wants to know if she'll have a job in Heaven. Her dream showed her checking a list as souls came. She viewed their talents and found jobs for them. The thing I did not know that came up in the dream was that she was trained in human resources. Perfect, I've often said that this life is a training ground for what we will do in Heaven. If we've totally missed our mark, we come back to do it over again and hope we do better the next time. Several past life experiences came to light in my book, *'When God Stood Up'*, which chronicles the majority of my dreams for others.

March 2, 2022

Yet another dream for another person. A lawyer came to our apartment complex, we met in the hall. I was introduced as the resident writer and we began talking about dreams. He told me of a past life experience he'd had. When he was about four or five, he told his parents that he was old before he was young. Trying to dig into the meaning of what he was saying, he'd talked about a confederate soldier in a graveyard. What would a child that young know about graveyards, or the Confederacy? He proceeded to draw a picture for them that they still have of a confederate soldier hiding behind a gravestone. He's lost the memory but the picture still exists. He has many dreams. One that has recurred over a long period of time is of being in a library. He takes a book off the shelf, opens it, and the book disappears in a puff into the ceiling-less sky above him.

Dream: The dream told us that he was to tell his story and his dreams before they disappeared. They are being given to him to share. The truth of his former life, showed to me, were two things in the dream. First was his newness to his office and the second was his interest in politics.

March 11, 2022

Dream: This dream told me that Jim was with me. He was to die on the twenty-first of the month. Today, in the dream, - it's the twentieth. We went to bed - but a light was shining in our eyes. I had trouble finding the switch to turn it off and the owner of the house it was coming from apologized for the inconvenience. (Could the light be the light of Heaven?) The next day, Jim dressed carefully and went to find a meadow full of flowers where he could lie down. After one try, he found a spot where he was comfortable.

Meaning: I believe I'm getting the story of his passing from his point of view. The weakness talked about in earlier dreams could be that he'd not found his place to lie down. The flowery meadow reminds me of the flowers in Holland.

Dream two: A second dream that same night had us looking for his mother in a museum. After asking for her, we were led to a narrow, steep staircase going down. She was hunting for war souvenirs. I said there was no way that I could manage those stairs, much less holding on to Jim, who was weak.

Meaning: Oma spent four years of her married life in Holland under German occupation. Father had been taken by the Germans and she had six children to care for. It was a major part of her life, and now that she was safe, she was looking for souvenirs. Jim and I were not going there.

March 12, 2022

Dream: I was to give a little boy a ride on a motorbike. I was new to this but gave it a try. We went to a big body of water and back. He wanted to go to England. It was getting dark. I said tomorrow. I wanted to go in the daylight so I could see where I was going.

Meaning: Now, looking back at this from the perspective of a few months and many dreams, I think, perhaps Jim was expecting me to show him around Heaven, take him to his mother as he would later do for me. I'm telling him that I can't see clearly. He'll have to wait. The motorbike (or motorcycle) was his favorite form of transportation.

March 13, 2022

Dream: I'm searching frantically for Jim. He has taken the whole front of our house away. His friend, Mike, is helping me in my search.

Meaning: A house, in a dream, represents a person's life. The whole front of mine has been taken away and my inner workings exposed. That seems to be what this writing is doing. I'm doing it for Jim, but he is doing it for me. Mike brings back memories from back when we owned a marina. He was Jim's best friend by far. We lost track of each other. Perhaps he is on the other side and helping me find Jim.

March 17, 2022

Dream: I go with the family to an amusement park. There I get separated from my family. I search, but can't find our car. I walk to the entrance and wait until I realize this is the wrong place. Then I walk to the exit. I'll see them as they leave. I wait but don't see them and I become frantic as I realize that I'm left alone. I awaken feeling frantic.

Meaning: I'm truly living my grief in my dreams. My frantic feeling when I wake is not anything like the calmness that fills my days as I write about the dreams in the Bible and about how I'm processing my grief through my dreams. I'm left behind, as Jim is gone and my children do not understand me and my penchant for dreams; the forty-plus years I've put into writing about them, teaching, lecturing about them. Jim lived it with me and now he's gone. I promised Him that I'd be all right and whenever I start to feel sorry for myself, I remember that promise and pick up my writing again.

March 27, 2022

My thoughts after the last revelation shook me to the core. They were all about getting on with writing the dreams down, so I could get on with something happier. Alas, this next dream just seems to rub the truth into me. I now know the physical effects of grief.

Dream: I lost my job, return home to find my roommates have thrown me out. I take my young son, my books and momentous and leave. He asks, "Where will we go, Mom?" I say "Grandma will take us in, like she did before." But I'm not so sure. Grandma is in Heaven.

Meaning: It's being told to me in another way that I've lost everything. Pardon the tears. I have my books. I try to picture us living with Gram. Maybe I should keep my eye on the big picture, my books and dream work. I immediately add the photos of my book covers to the list of things I want included in my Celebration of Life.

March 31, 2022

Dream: Jim and I are choosing new furniture for our home. We thought that we left the children behind, but they are there, choosing furniture for their rooms.

Meaning: Jim is visiting again, helping me to move ahead, choosing new furniture can mean a new way of thinking, a new plan of action. I'm changing the interior of my house, the house in a dream meaning 'me'. My thoughts, ideas, something along that line is changing and Jim is behind it. Has he become strong in Heaven? I hope so. Are the children going to go along with my new plan? One can only hope.

April 1, 2022

Dream: Surprise! I'm going to live with Gram. I rush out, not even packing. I stop at a store and buy the bare essentials enough to last three days. The store is closing, I look for a bus, but end up in a taxi. But while in the car, I question the driver's turns.

Meaning: Keep my eye on Heaven. I won't be going soon, as I'm given a time-line of three days. Three days have passed since that dream and I'm still on earth. It may have something to do with writing this book and my dream work for God. What decisions have come up. I've passed on a couple of promising advertising plans. I hate to think I passed on something that would get my work out to the public, but maybe I did. The taxi is me, again, and someone else is driving my life. I must stick to my own decisions as I'm afraid that the taxi driver is taking the wrong turns, symbolic of me making the wrong decisions.

April 2, 2022

Jim's back.

Dream: Jim and I are driving around and discover a new river. We can't see the other side. There's lots of rich farmland on our side. We stop at the only farmhouse we see. Surprise, it's someone we know! They've lived there a long time and they don't know what is on the other side of the river either.

Meaning: He's taking me to the edge of 'forever'. In reality, he knows what's on the other side but maybe there's a lot more to explore. He still wants to share everything with me. How sweet!

April 3, 2022

Dream: We've bought the top of a hill. There's lots of green grass that ends, at the bottom, at a lake so large you cannot see the other side even from the top of the hill. On the other side are mobile homes. Jim and I talk of further development. Jim leaves, and I realize I'm to do it alone.

Song: *Back In The Saddle Again*

Meaning: The mobile homes, I see, as temporary homes – as we are temporary on this earth. I'm to usher in more development. Is this family of mine to grow before I pass? After the dreams of everyone leaving me, this is a welcome idea. As for the song, if you look up the words, you'll see it's about freedom and choosing friends. Jim has sent this to me before. Perhaps he's telling me to enjoy my freedom. That made me laugh. That's good.

April 9, 2022

This night's dreams were the first to take me to Heaven and visit my relatives.

Dream: It was a special day, the kind where you visit family and bring them gifts. Jim took me to see where David Townsend lived (my nephew that passed in January) He lived in a one story-home that sat at the junction of two small rivers. He had a small rowboat with a motor that he used to travel in either direction he wanted, exploring the streams. (This is unlike the earthly David who collected Jeeps and ATV' S and many other expensive, motor-driven items). He is content and happy in this simple life. Perhaps he's learning a lesson that he hadn't learned on earth. I ask if we are going to see his father (my brother who passed in 1945). He says yes, but he has no present to take to him. Then we realize that my being there would be present enough! David was concerned about their acceptance, or lack thereof, of the woman in his house. I assured him we would accept both her and her beliefs.

Song: On waking this hymn was repeating in my head – *"It Is Well with My Soul."*

April 11, 2022

Two dreams this night that introduces us to my baby. I deny it at first, but finally accept the responsibility.

Dream: I drove my friends to work in a store. I wanted to stay and work, but knew that I had to get back home to take care of the baby, not my baby. I changed its diaper, made it a bottle and saw that Grandfather was awake. I put it in his arms. (If the baby is this book of grief dreams, I'm still expecting someone else to take care of it.

Although I know it's my duty.) I'm now looking for a playpen.

Dream Two: I went to the first day of school to teach a class. I asked the class to come up with three ways to move something, like moving a pencil to the teacher's desk. I explained I was a writer and had to get home to take care of a baby. (This is why I believe the baby is my writing about grief through dreams.)

Meaning; Perhaps there are three different ways to get this to a market that would appreciate it. Or will it take me three tries to get it published? Who knows? I'll just keep plugging along. One thing for sure, Jim is telling me to take care of our baby! This is when I began writing the dreams that were in my dream journal, our babies.

April 18, 2022

Dream: Jim has been sick but is feeling better. I start a list of things that I want him to do but the word is out and he's bombarded with requests for handyman work. My stuff will have to wait.

Dream number Two: It's been a tough day in the wedding planning business. Some wire we sold to the city to help hold up to bridges is rusting. We have lots more. We need to call the supplier and tell him about it.

Meaning: Two set-backs but I'm glad to know Jim is feeling better. Both a wedding and a bridge, in dreams, is a connection, a coming together. I can only hope. Getting rusty is a sign it's old.

April 19, 2022

Dream: Bridges again, different this time. Someone wants to tattoo a bridge on my nose. It is an American Indian honor. It looks like the top two sides if an equilateral triangle. It's secret meaning is that no one can hurt me. He whispers the meaning to me. No one can cross it.

Meaning: I'll leave that to your imagination.

Dream Number Two: I save the life of a lady giving a speech to a church group. She had been bitten by a poisonous spider. I'm given a check as a reward.

Meaning: Perhaps it was foretelling the Covid that I would get hit with soon. I got through it okay, lived to give another speech. Bit by the spider named Covid.

April 25, 2022

Dream: I'm preparing gifts for a family the exact same ages and gender as mine. My children give up one of their gifts each for them.

Meaning: Sometimes you can only guess. I'm giving away my own gifts (My dream work?). Perhaps I'm being told to get back into giving speeches. I'm in a new environment with many people who've not heard what I have to say. That day I began to look in the newspaper for a way to advertise, that's as far as I got.

April 28, 2022

Dream: I'm struggling with life issues like taxes. The authorities are arresting the man I work for. Where did he get the $798,000? I wanted to know, also. A car pulled up driven by my earthly father. Inside the open door was my grandmother. They wanted me to get in with them. I said, 'no, I have to hear the end of the story. Please wait.' I realized how much I loved and missed my father and grandmother. A feeling of great love washed over me.

Meaning: Some people believe that before you die, you are asked if you're ready to go yet. Dad and Gram were asking me and I said no, I wanted to hear the end of some story. I wondered if my dreams were taking a turn with this invitation. I love Dad and Gram but why didn't Jim come for me? Are we going separate ways in Heaven?

May 4, 2022

Dream: I'm back in a house with a woman who irons a lot. A man is there that I don't like. I make him go. Another man appears to be nicer until I find him in my bed. He has to go also. Meanwhile the lady keeps ironing and does not take responsibility for the men.

Meaning: This takes me back to my childhood in my mother's house. She worked hard, ironed a lot and brought several men 'friends' into the house. I was the one who had to leave. Was I seeing Mom in Heaven? Who knows?

Dream number three: that night I see a car that looks familiar and am delighted to see my father.

Meaning: In life, he did come for me just as I was trying to run away from Mom's house. I was age fourteen.

May 8, 20222

Dream: Jim and I live in an old messy camper. The table and other surfaces piled high with papers. An English lady comes and wants to buy one of my books. Then a man comes and wants to buy one of my books. Jim wants to know how they knew about them and I tell him of the promo in England and Australia. We celebrate and decide to buy a new larger camper.

Meaning: The promo is true and I think Jim and I were celebrating it in my dreams, the only way that I can reach him and he's the only one that I could celebrate this small victory. We felt rich enough to buy a bigger home. Perhaps the home signifies humbleness. We can expand our humbleness by indulging in a bigger temporary home. I might add, he's the only one that I could celebrate this small victory with. No one living would understand and he came in the night to do this for me. Love you, Jim.

May 13, 2022

Dream: Jim is leaving me. He's says that I've been neglecting him. Later in the dream I was ignoring our children even though I'd taken them fishing and picked up the hooks from the ground so no one would get hurt. The fishing was catch and release.

Meaning: It has been a few days since I bothered to write my dreams. I hope Jim comes back. The children in the dream, I believe are my projects, this recording of grief dreams and the documentary script that I'm writing. The third child could be the promoting that I could be doing on my own with the books. The hooks on the ground show that, on the ground (under my feet) they are on my mind and I can pick it up whenever I get the urge.

ABOUT THE AUTHOR

Carol Oschmann is the mother of three, grandmother of four, and great-grandmother of 5. Born in Rochester, NY. She met Jim when the church she and her grandmother attended, The First Dutch Reformed Church of Rochester NY, brought Jim and most of his family over from Holland as immigrants. His father had survived a German concentration camp.

Her dream life began as an adult and led to many healings. Her passion to help others led to the gift of being able to dream for other people's problems. *When God Stood Up* tells the story. She went on to write *Biblical Dream Study*, it finds lessons about our own dreams from the dreams of the Bible. She also has a MG book titled *Overboard on Lake Ontario*. Recently introduced is her book, *Finding Spirit in Prison Inmates Dreams*, chronicling her time spent teaching prison inmates in a Florida prison how to understand what their dreams were telling them.

Some books are on Amazon, for all plus *When God Stood Up* go to caroloschmann.com 12.99

She welcomes your comments. Email oschmann@verizon.net

CPSIA information can be obtained
at www.ICGtesting.com
Printed in the USA
JSHW041950161022
31406JS00003B/6

9 781958 554166